THE ULTIMATE
MINNESOTA VIKINGS
TRIVIA BOOK

A Collection of Amazing Trivia Quizzes
and Fun Facts for Die-Hard Vikings Fans!

Ray Walker

CONTENTS

INTRODUCTION

Obviously, you're forever inspired by your favorite team. In this case, the team in lights is none other than the Minnesota Vikings, founded in 1961, playing football in suburban Minneapolis, and surely one of the best teams in the entire history of the NFL. Although, fans of the archrival Green Bay Packers might want to argue over your claim just a bit.

The Twin Cities of Minneapolis and Saint Paul have long been host to exciting sports and winning pro teams: the Minnesota Twins in Major League Baseball, the Timberwolves in the National Basketball Association, the Minnesota Wild (formerly the North Stars) in the National Hockey League, the WNBA's Lynx, and Minnesota F.C. in Major League Soccer. Multinational companies like Best Buy, Cargill, Target, 3M, and the UnitedHealth Group make the pair of cities even more dynamic.

But your Minnesota Vikings are extra special. There's no place in the world to play and watch football like their unique home field, U.S. Bank Stadium, located in the Downtown East section of Minneapolis—especially when it's filled with 66,200 raucous Vikings fans.

This year, the Vikings will celebrate 61 years of existence at (or near!) the peak of the pro football world, and you'll be there, armed with all the trivia and fun facts on their colorful players, big signings and trades, and the incredible emotional highs and lows of a pro sports team. The Vikes have had more than their fair share, including the team's four runs to the Super Bowl (in 1970, 1974, 1975, and 1977). Yet they join the Buffalo Bills by falling in all four heartbreaking contests. But hope springs eternal in "The Land of 10,000 Lakes."

Clearly, you may use the book as you wish. Each chapter contains 20 quiz questions in a mix of multiple-choice and true-false formats, an answer key (Don't worry, it's on a separate page!), and a section of ten "Did You Know?" facts about the team.

For the record, the information and stats in this book are current up to the beginning of 2021. The Minnesota Vikings will surely break more records and win more awards as the seasons march on, so keep this in mind when you're watching the next game with your friends. You never quite know: someone could suddenly start a conversation with the phrase, "Did you know…?", and you'll be ready.

CHAPTER 1:

ORIGINS & HISTORY

QUIZ TIME!

1. One of the most colorful franchises in the history of the NFL (and not only because of their trademark purple and gold uniforms), in what year were the Vikings founded?

   a. 1957
   b. 1961
   c. 1965
   d. 1969

2. In which year did the Vikings win their one and only NFL championship?

   a. 1962
   b. 1965
   c. 1968
   d. 1969

3. Which coach that Minnesota hired in 1967 helped kick off the team's longest period of success?

   a. Bud Grant
   b. Dennis Green

c. Norm Van Brocklin

d. Mike Zimmer

4. In the 1970s, Minnesota's fearsome defensive line was nicknamed "the Purple People Eaters."

a. True

b. False

5. One famous Vikings quarterback was credited as a pioneer in making plays with his legs (i.e., scrambling). Who was he?

a. Brett Favre

b. Warren Moon

c. George Shaw

d. Fran Tarkenton

6. In 11 seasons, between 1968 and 1978, how many times did the Vikings qualify for the playoffs?

a. 4

b. 6

c. 8

d. 10

7. When an AFL franchise was first granted to the city of Minneapolis in 1959, which of the following businessmen was NOT involved in the deal?

a. Bill Boyer

b. Kirk Cousins

c. H.P. Skoglund

d. Max Winter

8. When Minnesota's ownership decided to give up their AFL membership in 1970, which of the NFL franchises did they become?

   a. 10th
   b. 12th
   c. 14th
   d. 17th

9. When the Vikes finally won their first division title in 1968, what was the name of their division?

   a. NFC North Division
   b. NFC Central Division
   c. Doomsday Division
   d. Great Lakes Division

10. Since their inception in 1961, how many victories have the Vikes racked up, as of 2020?

   a. 412
   b. 424
   c. 466
   d. 488

11. How many division titles have the Vikings won?

   a. 10
   b. 15
   c. 20
   d. 30

12. The Vikings have had 36 starting quarterbacks, and they've never had more than three starting quarterbacks in one season.

a. True

b. False

13. Which ancient region of the world did the original Vikings (who now adorn Minnesota's helmets) come from?

    a. Ireland

    b. The North Pole

    c. Russia

    d. Scandinavia

14. What was the name of the Minneapolis team that played on and off in the NFL in the 1920s and 1930s?

    a. Bulldogs

    b. Marines/Red Jackets

    c. Monsters

    d. Panhandlers

15. What was the name of the stadium in suburban Bloomington that the Vikes called home from 1961 to 1981?

    a. Hubert H. Humphrey Metrodome

    b. Metropolitan Stadium

    c. Parade Stadium

    d. TFC Bank Stadium

16. When the Vikings played and won their final home game in the Metrodome in 2013, which opponent did they beat, 14-13?

    a. Chicago Bears

    b. Cleveland Browns

c. Detroit Lions

d. Green Bay Packers

17. When the 1998 Minnesota squad scored a 15-1 regular-season record, they also piled up a then-record number of points in one campaign. How many?

a. 486

b. 512

c. 545

d. 556

18. From the beginning, in 1961, the Vikings launched an energetic marketing program resulting in first-year season ticket sales of nearly 26,000, and an average home attendance of 34,586, about 85% of Metropolitan Stadium's capacity of 40,800.

a. True

b. False

19. Early in 1961, Minnesota decided on its first head coach, Norm Van Brocklin, fresh off a championship win over Green Bay. Who did Norm play quarterback for at that time?

a. Dallas Cowboys

b. New York Giants

c. Philadelphia Eagles

d. St. Louis Rams

20. The most notable draft pick in 1961 was a youthful quarterback named Fran Tarkenton. What college had he played for?

a. University of Connecticut
b. University of Florida
c. University of Georgia
d. University of Tennessee

QUIZ ANSWERS

1. B – 1961

2. D – 1969

3. A – Bud Grant

4. A – True

5. D – Fran Tarkenton

6. D – 10

7. B – Kirk Cousins

8. C – 14th

9. B – NFC Central Division

10. D – 488

11. C – 20

12. B – False (The Vikings have had 39 starting quarterbacks in their history, and have never had more than three in any one season.)

13. D – Scandinavia

14. B – Marines/Red Jackets

15. B – Metropolitan Stadium

16. C – Detroit Lions

17. D – 556

18. A – True

19. C – Philadelphia Eagles

20. C – University of Georgia

DID YOU KNOW?

1. The ravenous defensive line that the Vikings featured in the 1970s produced two Hall-of-Famers: Carl Eller and Alan Page.

2. In 1969, Minnesota's dominant defense led them to a league championship, the last NFL championship before the merger of the NFL with the AFL.

3. Minnesota is the most successful NFL franchise to have never won a Super Bowl. The franchise ranks sixth all-time in win percentage, and seventh overall in combined regular season and postseason wins.

4. The Vikings are one of only three teams, together with the Pittsburgh Steelers and Los Angeles Rams, to appear in at least one conference title game in every decade since the 1970s.

5. In the early 1960s, Ole Haugsrud was added to Minnesota's team ownership. When he sold his Duluth Eskimos franchise back to the league in the 1920s, the agreement permitted him to own 10% of any future Minnesota team.

6. As of 2019, the Vikes have won at least three games in every season except 1962, and they are one of only seven NFL teams to win at least 15 games in a single regular season.

7. The search for the team's first head coach led to a secret visit by Ara Parseghian, then at Northwestern and later the big boss at Notre Dame. His cover was blown by the local press, forcing him to deny the clandestine meeting.

8. The Vikes won their first-ever regular-season game, defeating the Chicago Bears, 37-13, on Opening Day 1961. Tarkenton came off the bench to toss four touchdown passes and run for another to lead the upset.

9. Harold "Bud" Grant Jr. served as the head coach of the Vikings in the NFL for 18 seasons, leading the franchise to four Super Bowls in the '70s.

10. Before taking Minnesota's reins, Grant was the head coach of the Winnipeg Blue Bombers in the Canadian Football League for ten seasons, winning the Grey Cup four times.

CHAPTER 2:

THE NUMBERS GAME

QUIZ TIME!

1. Kicker Fred Cox is the all-time leading scorer for the Vikings. Out of the 539 extra points he attempted, how many did he miss?

   a. 10
   b. 14
   c. 20
   d. 36

2. The Minnesota franchise has retired six numbers. Which of the following players is NOT one of them?

   a. Cris Carter (#80)
   b. Alan Page (#88)
   c. Adrian Peterson (#28)
   d. Fran Tarkenton (#10)

3. Created by Doug Drinen (PFR founder), the Approximate Value (AV) method is an attempt to put a single number on the seasonal value of a player at any position from any

year (starting in 1950). The all-time AV leader for Minnesota is center Mike Tingelhoff at 182.

a. True

b. False

4. One opponent in particular dreads playing Minnesota because the Vikes boast a .664 winning percentage against them. Which team?

a. Chicago Bears

b. Detroit Lions

c. Green Bay Packers

d. Jacksonville Jaguars

5. The biggest comeback ever in Minnesota history came in a 28-27 victory over the San Francisco 49ers in 1977. How many points were the Vikes behind at one point in the game?

a. 27

b. 24

c. 22

d. 20

6. On the other hand, Minnesota was ahead by 21 points in a game on December 24, 1995, before diabolically losing, 24-27. Who was the lucky foe?

a. Cincinnati Bengals

b. Dallas Cowboys

c. Houston Texans

d. San Diego Chargers

7. In the first game ever played at the Hubert H. Humphrey Metrodome in 1982, the Vikings squeaked past the Seahawks. What was the final tally in that low-scoring affair?

    a. 6-2
    b. 7-3
    c. 9-6
    d. 10-7

8. The most points ever scored in a single game by a Vikings team was in a win over the Dallas Cowboys in 1970. How many points did Minnesota put on the board?

    a. 48
    b. 49
    c. 54
    d. 60

9. The Vikings ripped off 13 consecutive regular-season wins in one particular campaign. Which season was it?

    a. 1998-99
    b. 1985-86
    c. 1978-79
    d. 1974-75

10. The 1998 team was on fire offensively, scoring a record number of touchdowns. How many did they rack up?

    a. 59
    b. 64
    c. 68
    d. 76

11. The career leader for Minnesota in quarterback rating for passing is Kirk Cousins at 103.6. Which quarterback ranks second at 91.5?

    a. Daunte Culpepper
    b. Brad Johnson
    c. Tommy Kramer
    d. Wade Wilson

12. Which of the following Vikings running backs leads the franchise in rushing attempts (2,418), yards gained (11,747), and touchdowns (97)?

    a. Bill Brown
    b. Dalvin Cook
    c. Chuck Foreman
    d. Adrian Peterson

13. Cris Carter holds numerous Vikings receiving records. How many receptions did he grab in both the 1994 and 1995 seasons to set the franchise mark?

    a. 129
    b. 122
    c. 115
    d. 110

14. Randy Moss twice hauled in 17 touchdown passes in a single season with Minnesota: in 1998 and 2003. For which other team did he record 23 touchdown catches in 2007?

    a. Buffalo Bills
    b. Miami Dolphins

c. New England Patriots

d. Oakland Raiders

15. "The Minneapolis Miracle" (or "Minnesota Miracle") saw the Vikings score on a 61-yard touchdown pass with 25 seconds left to nip the New Orleans Saints (who had taken the lead after recovering from a 17-0 first-half deficit) on January 14, 2018.

a. True

b. False

16. The first Viking ever elected to the Hall of Fame was master quarterback Fran Tarkenton. In what year?

a. 1976

b. 1980

c. 1986

d. 1992

17. Which Minnesota running back was the first to rush for 100 or more yards in a game, versus the Los Angeles Rams back in 1961?

a. Raymond Hayes

b. Mike Morris

c. Robert Smith

d. Scott Studwell

18. When the Vikings upset their rivals from Chicago, 37-13, in their first-ever regular-season game in 1961, who scored the team's first points ever on a 12-yard field goal?

a. Morten Andersen

b. Fred Cox

c. Ryan Longwell

d. Mike Mercer

19. When quarterback Fran Tarkenton was named league MVP in 1975 while leading the Vikes to a regular-season mark of 12-2, how many interceptions did he throw to go along with 25 touchdown tosses?

a. 6

b. 9

c. 13

d. 19

20. In 20 seasons, head coach Bud Grant led Minnesota to 12 playoff appearances, 11 division titles, and four Super Bowls. His career regular-season record was 151-87-5 (.632).

a. True

b. False

QUIZ ANSWERS

1. C – 20

2. C – Adrian Peterson (#28)

3. A – True

4. B – Detroit Lions

5. B – 24

6. A – Cincinnati Bengals

7. B – 7-3

8. C – 54

9. D – 1974-75

10. B – 64

11. A – Daunte Culpepper

12. D – Adrian Peterson

13. B – 122

14. C – New England Patriots

15. A – True

16. C – 1986

17. A – Raymond Hayes

18. D – Mike Mercer

19. C – 13

20. B – False (Grant coached Minnesota for 17 seasons.)

DID YOU KNOW?

1. In 2012, Adrian Peterson considered changing his jersey number from 23 to 28, until he was informed he'd have to pay for all the new jerseys produced (totaling a cool $1 million).

2. At one point in the 2020 season, Vikings running back Dalvin Cook's 16 rushing scores put him ahead of 19 NFL teams for total rushing touchdowns.

3. In a game against the St. Louis Rams in Week 15 of 2012, Blair Walsh equaled the NFL record for field goals made from 50 yards or more with his eighth kick (a new team mark). His three 50-yarders in the contest was also a team record.

4. In addition to his scrambling prowess, Fran Tarkenton liked to air it out, passing for 33,098 yards in his 11 years with the Vikings.

5. "The Minnesota Miracle" game in January 2018 was the first in the history of the NFL playoffs to end in a touchdown as time expired.

6. As of the end of 2020, playing under head coach Mike Zimmer, the Vikings have a win-loss record of 18-2 (.900) when they receive the ball to start the second half and score on that drive. This means they win 90% of the time in such situations.

7. Named one of "The 30 Greatest Vikings," Bill Brown ran the ball for 5,757 yards and gained 3,177 in the air, totaling 8,934 offensive yards. He added 52 touchdowns on the ground, 23 through the air, and one touchdown on a kick return.

8. On December 15, 1968, the Vikes beat the Philadelphia Eagles, 24-17, at Franklin Field and then holed up in their dressing room to listen to the Chicago-Green Bay game on the radio. Minnesota needed the Bears to lose to clinch Minnesota's first division title. Chicago tried to come back from a 28-10 deficit, but finally fell 28-17.

9. In 1971, Alan Page became the first defensive player to be named the MVP of the NFL by the Associated Press. Page guided a Vikings defense that held opponents to fewer than 10 points per game to lead the league in scoring defense for the third straight year.

10. Vikings' Offensive Coordinator Bill Billick seems by consensus one of the best ever. In the 1998 season alone, his purple team scored a team record (until 2007 at least) number of points (556), together with the most yards from scrimmage in a single season (6,424), and most points per game (34.8). /
https://www.dailynorseman.com/2017/9/7/16269674/by-the-numbers-offensive-coordinator

CHAPTER 3:

CALLING THE SIGNALS

QUIZ TIME!

1. Fran Tarkenton normally heads the conversation as Minnesota's greatest-ever quarterback, launching 239 touchdown passes, 80 more than the next in line. Who was the runner-up?

   a. Brett Favre
   b. Tommy Kramer
   c. Warren Moon
   d. Wade Wilson

2. Tarkenton passed for 47,003 yards in his career, which still stands 13th in NFL history. Which of the following signal-callers is NOT ahead of him?

   a. Tom Brady
   b. Drew Brees
   c. Peyton Manning
   d. Vinny Testaverde

3. At the same time that Tarkenton was drafted by Minnesota in 1961, he was also selected by an AFL team. Which AFL franchise wanted the Tark as well?

   a. Boston Patriots
   b. Buffalo Bills
   c. Houston Oilers
   d. New York Titans

4. Despite Daunte Culpepper's tendency to cough the ball up, he was one of Minnesota's all-time best quarterbacks. What injury required surgery and effectively ended his career as a Viking in 2005?

   a. Knee
   b. Neck
   c. Shoulder
   d. Toe

5. Culpepper scrambled for numerous big gains and touchdowns as the Vikings' signal-caller from 1999 to 2005. How many fumbles did he lose (which is still a franchise record)?

   a. 65
   b. 74
   c. 81
   d. 99

6. It would be hard for any Vikings quarterback to outdo Tommy Kramer's achievement in his 1977 debut against Jim Plunkett and the 49ers. After trailing by 24 points,

how many touchdown passes did Kramer fire in the last-minute win?

    a. 6

    b. 5

    c. 4

    d. 3

7. Joe Kapp played with Minnesota for a mere three years. But he set an NFL record (at the time in 1969) with seven touchdown passes in a single game. Who was the hapless opponent?

    a. Baltimore Colts

    b. Houston Texans

    c. New York Giants

    d. San Diego Chargers

8. According to one writer, Kapp makes the list of all-time greatest Minnesota quarterbacks because of his "_____, determination, and leadership." What's missing?

    a. Arm

    b. Grit

    c. Hustle

    d. Uncanny speed

9. Brett Favre came to Minnesota from rival Green Bay in 2009 and proceeded to have the best season of his illustrious career. He led the Vikes to a 12-4 record and a place in the NFC Championship game. He racked up a quarterback rating of 107.2 while tossing 33 touchdowns against only seven interceptions.

a. True

b. False

10. That same year, the Vikings and Favre lost to the New Orleans Saints in overtime in the NFC Championship game. The game acquired an unusual nickname after Saints players and coaches were suspended a full three years later. What was the game named?

a. Bountygate

b. Deflategate

c. Inflategate

d. Watergate

11. After an injury in the 1996 season, Warren Moon refused to take a $3.8 million pay cut to serve as Minnesota's backup quarterback the next season. Who was given the starting job at that time?

a. Jeff George

b. Brad Johnson

c. Bob Lee

d. Jim McMahon

12. Brad Johnson is notable for making NFL history in Minnesota's 1997 game against the Tennessee Titans in which he became the first NFL player to complete a touchdown pass to himself.

a. True

b. False

13. In 1985, even though Wade Wilson was diagnosed with a type of diabetes, he led the Vikes to one of the greatest

comeback wins in franchise victory. After trailing 23-0 in the fourth quarter, what was the final score as Minnesota beat the Eagles?

a. 32-30

b. 30-27

c. 28-23

d. 24-23

14. Wilson later became the Chicago Bears' quarterbacks coach from 2004 to 2006 and helped one quarterback have his best season ever while taking the Bears to Super Bowl XLI. Who was the Bear in question?

a. Chris Chandler

b. Rex Grossman

c. Kyle Orton

d. Kordell Stewart

15. The team that originally drafted Rich Gannon envisioned turning him into a running back. Rich balked at the idea and was soon traded to the Vikings. Which was the former franchise?

a. Green Bay Packers

b. Miami Dolphins

c. New England Patriots

d. New York Jets

16. Minnesota backup Bob Lee led the Vikes to a 1977 divisional round win over the Rams, 14-7, after an injury to Tarkenton. Why was the game considered "infamous"?

a. Muddy conditions

b. Power outage

c. Rainy conditions

d. Snowy conditions

17. "General" Lee had a successful stint with another team, which knocked off the 9-0 Minnesota Vikings in 1973. Which team was it?

a. Atlanta Falcons

b. Houston Oilers

c. San Francisco 49ers

d. St. Louis Rams

18. When quarterback Kirk Cousins couldn't agree to terms with the Washington Redskins, he signed a free-agent deal with Minnesota in 2018. What was the guaranteed amount Kirk received for three years?

a. $45 million

b. $60 million

c. $74 million

d. $84 million

19. Cousins signed a $66 million contract extension in 2020, but in a 28-11 loss against the Indianapolis Colts, he threw for only 113 yards and three interceptions, resulting in the third-lowest quarterback rating in franchise history. What was his rating?

a. 15.9

b. 28.6

c. 37.5

d. 57.7

20. Sam Bradford was acquired by Minnesota in 2016 for two draft picks, and he helped lead the Vikings to their first win in the new indoor U.S. Bank Stadium over the Packers. Which injured quarterback did he replace?

a. Teddy Bridgewater

b. Gus Frerotte

c. Christian Ponder

d. Spergon Wynn

QUIZ ANSWERS

1. B – Tommy Kramer

2. D – Vinny Testaverde

3. A – Boston Patriots

4. A – Knee

5. C – 81

6. C – 4

7. A – Baltimore Colts

8. B – Grit

9. A – True

10. A – Bountygate

11. B – Brad Johnson

12. B – False (In fact, Johnson completed the touchdown pass to himself against the Carolina Panthers in 1997.)

13. C – 28-23

14. B – Rex Grossman

15. C – New England Patriots

16. A – Muddy conditions

17. A – Atlanta Falcons

18. D – $84 million

19. A – 15.9

20. A – Teddy Bridgewater

DID YOU KNOW?

1. After his football career, Fran Tarkenton was a commentator on *Monday Night Football* and a co-host of *That's Incredible!*. He also founded Tarkenton Software, a computer-program generator company, and he toured the U.S. promoting computer-aided software engineering (CASE).

2. After his 2005 injury, Daunte Culpepper bounced around a bit in stints with the Miami Dolphins, Oakland Raiders, and Detroit Lions. His pro career ended after one season with the Sacramento Mountain Lions of the United Football League (UFL).

3. Kramer earned the nickname "Two-Minute Tommy" for his ability to engineer comebacks. He led the Vikings to 19 comebacks (including one in the playoffs), with 15 in the fourth quarter. In 1980 and 1985, Kramer had four in each season.

4. In a 1980 game later called "The Miracle at The Met," Kramer was part of an iconic moment for the Vikings. He threw a game-winning Hail Mary touchdown pass to a covered Ahmad Rashād with six seconds left. The Vikes trailed 23-9 in the fourth, but Kramer threw three touchdowns in the quarter.

5. When Joe Kapp was called to the podium to receive the team MVP award after the 1969 season, he famously

refused to accept. He claimed there were 40 MVP's on the Minnesota roster, and that "no one player should be put above the team."

6. In the spring of 1995, Brad Johnson joined the London Monarchs of the World League, an American football league in Europe. He led all WL quarterbacks in completions and earned 12,000 British pounds.

7. In his glorious 1998 campaign, Randall Cunningham led the league with a 106.0 passer rating while the Vikings piled up a then-NFL record 556 points, making him the first black quarterback to lead the league in the former category.

8. "When Randall came into the league... he was just different. He was so athletic. That's what you have to understand. There just weren't guys like Randall. The way he could run. The way he could throw. He brought something that a lot of people hadn't seen," exclaimed rival quarterback Doug Williams.

9. In September 2007, Wade Wilson was suspended for five games and fined $100,000 for buying and using performance-enhancing drugs. In his own defense, Wilson said that the drug (HGH) was needed to help his problem with diabetes. His toe was later amputated due to his struggles with diabetes.

10. Rich Gannon first played as a punter before switching to quarterback in his sophomore year with the University of Delaware Fightin' Blue Hens. He set 21 school records

there, including total offense (7,432 yards), passing yards (5,927), pass attempts (845), and completions (462).

CHAPTER 4:

BETWEEN THE TACKLES

QUIZ TIME!

1. In 2004, Adrian Peterson became the first college freshman ever to finish second in the Heisman Trophy voting. Which university did he play for?

   a. Florida Seminoles
   b. Nebraska Cornhuskers
   c. Oklahoma Sooners
   d. Penn State Nittany Lions

2. As a Minnesota rookie, Peterson romped for a record number of yards in a single 2007 game. How many did he gain in that contest against the San Diego Chargers?

   a. 201
   b. 225
   c. 278
   d. 296

3. Peterson snagged his third rushing title with Minnesota in 2015. Who was the last player to win a third such title, in 1996?

a. Jerome Bettis

b. Terrell Davis

c. Barry Sanders

d. Ricky Watters

4. Chuck Foreman started in three Super Bowls with the Vikings and was the team's premier running back for the franchise for most of the 1970s. What skill was he best known for as a back?

a. Blocking

b. Faking

c. Pass-catching

d. Punting

5. What nickname did Foreman earn for his slippery running style?

a. The Artful Dodger

b. The Jersey Juker

c. The Spin City Kid

d. The Spin Doctor

6. Vikings running back Robert Smith was the winner of the Mr. Football Award for two straight seasons (1988 and 1989) in high school. In which state did he play?

a. Alabama

b. Connecticut

c. Georgia

d. Ohio

7. As a running back, Darrin Nelson was a threat as both a runner and a receiver. However, he's perhaps best known

for dropping the game-tying touchdown on a fourth down in the closing moments of the 1987 NFC Championship game versus Washington.

a. True

b. False

8. Nelson participated in a bitter contract holdout in 1989, lost his starting spot to T.J. Dozier, and then was part of a monster trade for another highly touted runner. Who was Minnesota's fleet-footed trade target?

a. Ottis Anderson

b. Dalton Hilliard

c. Christian Okoye

d. Herschel Walker

9. Vikings running back Ted Brown's son J.T. also played a professional sport in Minnesota. For which team did he suit up?

a. Minnesota Timberwolves

b. Minnesota Twins

c. Minnesota United F.C.

d. Minnesota Wild

10. Mewelde Moore, Minnesota runner and returner, holds the Vikings' record with an average of 10.5 yards per punt return. He also has two of the 10 longest punt returns in team history. Each went for how many yards?

a. 54

b. 62

c. 71

d. 82

11. After being drafted by the Vikings in 2003, runner Onterrio Smith shaved "S.O.D." on the side of his head. What did the acronym stand for?

    a. Score On Delivery
    b. Special Of the Draft
    c. Steal Of the Draft
    d. Sudden Offensive Detonation

12. A Minnesota writer wrote that Dave Osborn was a Viking through and through. He played in foul weather and "was known more for his _____ than talent." What's missing?

    a. Determination
    b. Hard-headedness
    c. Muscles
    d. Toughness

13. Never a flashy player, Bill Brown had a no-nonsense running style that was a perfect fit for the Vikings teams of the 1960s and '70s. What was his nickname?

    a. Bad Billy
    b. Boom Boom
    c. Bruisin' Bill
    d. Buckin' Bill

14. Chuck Foreman's best year was in 1975 when he scored a then-record 22 touchdowns as a Viking. What was the record-breaking number of passes he caught that season?

a. 56

b. 66

c. 73

d. 87

15. This rusher's 95-yard touchdown scamper in 2006 from scrimmage was the longest in franchise history. What was the name of this rapid Minnesota running back?

a. Terry Allen

b. Bill Bennett

c. Clinton Jones

d. Chester Taylor

16. In six seasons (from 1961 to 1966) with the Vikings, Tommy Mason rushed for 3,252 yards and scored 28 touchdowns. How many yards did he gain afterward in four years as a Ram?

a. 1,626

b. 1,311

c. Less than 900

d. Less than 500

17. In his nine seasons in the NFL (1975 to 1983), including six with the Vikings, Rickey Young did not miss a single game, appearing in all 131 contests that his teams played in that span.

a. True

b. False

18. In 2018, Dalvin Cook finished the season with 615 yards gained, outdoing his backup, although he had fewer carries, and two touchdowns scored. Who was the other ball carrier behind him?

    a. Terry Allen
    b. Jerick McKinnon
    c. Latavius Murray
    d. Moe Williams

19. Tony Richardson is considered one of the best fullbacks in NFL history. In how many consecutive seasons did he lead the blocking for a runner gaining more than 1,000 yards (including Adrian Peterson)?

    a. 5
    b. 6
    c. 7
    d. 9

20. What was the name given by *USA Today* to honor hard-working and under-recognized players like H-back Jim Kleinsasser?

    a. All-Joe Team
    b. All Underrated Team
    c. G.I. Joe Team
    d. Hard-Working Hank Team

QUIZ ANSWERS

1. C – Oklahoma Sooners

2. D – 296

3. C – Barry Sanders

4. C – Pass-catching

5. D – The Spin Doctor

6. D – Ohio

7. A – True

8. D – Herschel Walker

9. D – Minnesota Wild

10. C – 71

11. C – Steal Of the Draft

12. D – Toughness

13. B – Boom Boom

14. C – 73

15. D – Chester Taylor

16. C – Less than 900

17. A – True

18. C – Latavius Murray

19. D – 9

20. A – All-Joe Team

DID YOU KNOW?

1. Following Adrian Peterson's record performance as a rookie in 2007, Deion Sanders, an NFL Network analyst, said: "He has the vision of a Marshall Faulk, the power of an Earl Campbell, and the speed of an Eric Dickerson. Let's pray he has the endurance of an Emmitt Smith."

2. When the Vikings lost Super Bowl VIII 24-7, Chuck Foreman was held to only 18 yards rushing and 27 yards receiving in the game. A year after Miami had gone undefeated, Foreman claimed the Dolphins were the best team that Minnesota faced in the Super Bowl that decade.

3. As part of Minnesota's 50th anniversary celebration, Foreman was named one of the 50 Greatest Vikings in 2010.

4. Though Robert Smith suffered from a number of injuries in his first few seasons, he finally broke out in 1997 with 1,266 yards rushing. Smith's finest pro year came in 2000 at the age of 28 when he led the NFC in rushing with 1,521 yards. Despite being at his peak, he retired after the season.

5. Darrin Nelson was truly a dual threat as a rusher and receiver with the Stanford Cardinals under Bill Walsh, becoming the first player in NCAA history to rush for more than 1,000 yards and catch more than 50 passes in a single season. He achieved that feat three times.

6. Born on March 3, 1962, Herschel Walker had some success as a pro football player, bobsledder, track sprinter, and mixed martial artist.

7. In December 1981, running back Ted Brown accidentally shot himself while handling a loaded revolver. The resulting injury required surgery to remove bullet and wood fragments from his thigh. There was a question about whether he would be able to continue his football career.

8. Mewelde Moore joined Onterrio Smith as the only Vikings rookies in franchise history to rush for consecutive 100-yard games in 2004. They were later joined by Adrian Peterson in 2007.

9. Bill Brown played in more games than any other running back in team history during his 13-year career. He carried the ball more often, was named to four Pro Bowls for his efforts, and is still a legend among Vikings fans.

10. Robert Smith still holds the Minnesota record for most rushing yards in a playoff game, with 140 against Dallas in 2000. Smith also set the record for most consecutive rushing attempts without a fumble, with 478.

CHAPTER 5:

CATCHING THE BALL

QUIZ TIME!

1. Randy Moss started on the right foot for the Vikings. How many touchdown passes did he catch in his rookie year (1998)?

   a. 12
   b. 15
   c. 17
   d. 20

2. Moss became well known for coming down with the majority of contested catches he went for. What phrase has entered football vernacular as a result of his rough treatment of defensive backs?

   a. Getting fleeced
   b. Getting juiced
   c. Getting mossed
   d. Getting randied

3. Cris Carter recovered from a bout with substance abuse but was forced out of Philly, and then he really broke out as a Vikings receiver. In what year was he enshrined in the Hall of Fame?

   a. 1995
   b. 1999
   c. 2010
   d. 2013

4. Which well-known ESPN broadcaster quipped about Cris Carter: "All he does is catch touchdowns."?

   a. Chris Berman
   b. Todd Blackledge
   c. Tim Hasselbeck
   d. Bob Ley

5. "Willie" Jake Reed ranked second in the NFL in receiving yards in the 1996 season, with 1,320. Who was first with 1,338 yards?

   a. Isaac Bruce
   b. Irving Fryar
   c. Herman Moore
   d. Jerry Rice

6. Receiver Sammy White played at Grambling University in Louisiana from 1972 to 1975 together with a future Super Bowl MVP. Who was he?

   a. Ottis Anderson
   b. Richard Dent

c. Jerry Rice

d. Doug Williams

7. Paul Flatley caught passes for the Vikings from 1963 to 1967. After retiring, he was a member of college football radio broadcasts for many years. For which team?

a. Ohio State Buckeyes

b. Michigan Wolverines

c. Minnesota Golden Gophers

d. North Dakota State Bison

8. In 2009, this Vikings receiver became the first ever to record three touchdowns, including a 101-yard kickoff return, in his first three games. Who was he?

a. Dalvin Cook

b. Jim Gilliam

c. Percy Harvin

d. Gene Washington

9. In 1972, Viking John Gilliam led the NFL in yards per catch, and finished second in receiving yards (1,035) and receiving yards per game (73.9). How many yards did he average per catch?

a. 14

b. 14

c. 20

d. 22

10. Besides the "The Miracle Catch" of a Hail Mary chuck by Tommy Kramer in 1980, Ahmad Rashād also has the

distinction of the longest play from scrimmage that didn't score a touchdown: 98 yards in a 1972 contest against the Rams.

a. True
b. False

11. Gene Washington took full advantage of his size (6'3" and 205 lbs./190.5 cm and 93 kg) to catch the football in the '60s for the Vikings and Broncos. In what track event was he the NCAA Indoor Champion in 1965 at Michigan State?

a. 50-yard dash
b. 60-yard hurdles
c. High jump
d. Steeplechase

12. Which Canadian Football League team did Leo Lewis play for immediately before coming to the Vikings as a receiver in 1981?

a. Edmonton Eskimos
b. Hamilton Tiger-Cats
c. Ottawa Rough Riders
d. Winnipeg Blue Bombers

13. Anthony Carter's 45-yard touchdown catch and dash against Indiana as time ran out to give the University of Michigan a 27-21 victory is considered one of the greatest plays in Michigan football history. Who made the frantic radio call on that fateful day?

a. Ford Bond

b. Howard Cosell

c. Bob Uecker

d. Bob Ufer

14. The number of all-purpose yards that Anthony Carter gained as a Viking in the 1987 playoffs remains a postseason NFL record. How many yards did he have?

    a. 466

    b. 543

    c. 642

    d. 711

15. Bisi Johnson filled in admirably for injured wideout Adam Thielen in 2019. What does his first name "Obalisi" mean in Nigerian (where his father came from)?

    a. "Bring honor to your family."

    b. "Bring prosperity to your family."

    c. "Honor your ancestors with hard work."

    d. "Honor your homeland with your actions."

16. Chad Beebe played high school ball for his famous father at the Aurora Christian Schools in Buffalo, New York. What's his dad's first name?

    a. Allen

    b. Don

    c. Mike

    d. Seth

17. In Week 12 of the 2020 season, Beebe scored a late go-ahead touchdown, which was the first touchdown of his

career, on a 10-yard reception from Kirk Cousins to guarantee a 28-27 victory. Who was the opponent that day?

a. Carolina Panthers
b. Dallas Cowboys
c. Miami Dolphins
d. Tennessee Titans

18. Since Randy Moss in 1988, Stefon Diggs was the first Vikings rookie to record consecutive 100-yard games and 80 or more receiving yards in his first three games.

a. True
b. False

19. Adam Thielen grew up in Detroit Lakes, Minnesota, idolizing Cris Carter and Randy Moss and wearing their Vikings jerseys as a kid. What's his NFL record for most receptions in the first half of a season?

a. 68
b. 74
c. 80
d. 91

20. At the 2009 NFL Scouting Combine, receiver Mike Wallace clocked an impressive time in the 40-yard dash. What was his mark?

a. 4.22 seconds
b. 4.33 seconds
c. 4.38 seconds
d. 4.52 seconds

QUIZ ANSWERS

1. C – 17

2. C – Getting mossed

3. D – 2013

4. A – Chris Berman

5. A – Isaac Bruce

6. D – Doug Williams

7. C – Minnesota Golden Gophers

8. C – Percy Harvin

9. D – 22

10. A – True

11. B – 60-yard hurdles

12. B – Hamilton Tiger-Cats

13. D – Bob Ufer

14. C – 642

15. B – "Bring prosperity to your family."

16. B – Don

17. A – Carolina Panthers

18. B – False (Randy Moss did it as a rookie in 1998.)

19. B – 74

20. B – 4.33 seconds

DID YOU KNOW?

1. Randy Moss still holds the single-season record for touchdown receptions, with 23. During his career, he led the NFL in touchdowns five times and had 10 seasons with 1,000 or more yards.

2. Cris Carter was released by Philly's Buddy Ryan in 1989 due to off-the-field issues. He was signed by the Vikings and turned his life and career around, becoming a two-time First Team and one-time Second Team All-Pro while playing in eight consecutive Pro Bowls.

3. In 1994, Jake Reed combined with teammate Cris Carter for 207 receptions, which was an NFL record at the time. Carter and Reed were also the first pair of teammates to amass 1,000 yards each in four consecutive seasons.

4. Ahmad Rashād originally failed the Vikings' physical in 1976 but was kept on the team at the insistence of quarterback Fran Tarkenton. The Vikings made it back to the Super Bowl at the end of that season, their most recent appearance to date.

5. One of the most spectacular, ferocious hits in NFL history happened to Sammy White during Super Bowl XI on January 9, 1977, at the Rose Bowl in Pasadena, California. The Raiders' Jack Tatum's tackle knocked White's chin strap off, and his helmet soared almost 10 yards. Luckily,

White returned to the game and ended up as Minnesota's leading receiver, though they lost.

6. On January 6, 2010, the Associated Press announced Percy Harvin's selection as the AP Offensive Rookie of the Year. He became the sixth Vikings player to win the award, joining Adrian Peterson (2007), Randy Moss (1998), Sammy White (1976), Chuck Foreman (1973), and Paul Flatley (1963).

7. After leaving Minnesota, John Gilliam became even more famous for returning the opening kickoff 94 yards in the New Orleans Saints' inaugural game in 1967 against the Los Angeles Rams for the first touchdown in New Orleans franchise history.

8. Gene Washington is the subject of the documentary *Through the Banks of the Red Cedar*, written and directed by his daughter Maya Washington.

9. Hassan Ameer Jones had his best season as a Vike in 1990 when he had 51 receptions for 810 yards and seven touchdowns.

10. After retiring from active play, Leo Lewis continued in the position of director of player development for the Vikings from 1992 to 2005. At the same time, Lewis wrote, edited, and published the Vikings' player and alumni newsletter.

CHAPTER 6:

TRENCH WARFARE

QUIZ TIME!

1. Henry Thomas was a mainstay on the Vikings' defensive line from 1987 to 1994. What was the nickname that Minnesota fans affectionately bestowed on him?

   a. Hammerin' Hank
   b. Hardware Hank
   c. Tacklin' Thomas
   d. Too Tough Thomas

2. Douglas Sutherland was a member of the notorious Purple People Eaters defensive line from 1971 to 1980. Which player did he normally fill in for in 1975?

   a. Carl Eller
   b. Gary Larsen
   c. Jim Marshall
   d. Alan Page

3. What was the motto of the infamous Minnesota tackling gang known as "the Purple People Eaters"?

a. "Dine on the quarterback"

b. "Eat anything that carries a football"

c. "Eat or be eaten"

d. "Meet at the quarterback"

4. Not only was Alan Page one of the most feared pass rushers of all time, but he served as a distinguished judge as well after football. What award was he the first defensive player ever to win?

a. Most Sportsmanlike Player

b. Most Valuable Player

c. Presidential Medal of Freedom

d. Vince Lombardi Trophy

5. At one point, Page played in a ridiculous number of games without an absence. How many?

a. 155

b. 189

c. 218

d. 241

6. As a left defensive end, and heralded member of the Purple People Eaters, Carl Eller was one of a select group of players to participate in all four of Minnesota's Super Bowls. How many were in that group?

a. 7

b. 11

c. 15

d. 17

7. Jim Marshall scooped up a record number of fumbles in his career. How many?

    a. 20
    b. 25
    c. 30
    d. 40

8. Despite Marshall's mistake in running 66 yards the wrong way, the Vikings won the game 27-22. Marshall soon received a letter from Roy Riegels, also infamous for a wrong-way run in the 1929 Rose Bowl. It said, "Welcome to the club." In 2019, Marshall's mishap was ranked number 54 among the NFL's 100 Greatest Plays.

    a. True
    b. False

9. Gary Larsen was called "the Policeman" because he mainly defended against the run for the Purple People Eaters. What was the name of his Minnesota college?

    a. Concordia College
    b. Macalester College
    c. Minnesota State
    d. Winona State

10. Kevin Williams was joined by Pat Williams (no relation) to form the "Williams Wall" and prevent opposing runners from getting far, from 2006 to 2008. What was another nickname given to the tandem?

    a. We Will Rock You Wall
    b. Williams Tag Team Wrestlers

c. Williams Undertakers

d. Williams Wrecking Crew

11. Jared Allen set the Vikings franchise record for most regular-season sacks in 2011. How many times that year did Allen wrap up opposing quarterbacks?

    a. 15

    b. 22

    c. 28

    d. 37

12. When Minnesota decided to switch to a 4-3 defense in the 1987 season, Chris Doleman moved from outside linebacker to the defensive line. What was his new position when he started to go sack-happy?

    a. Defensive end

    b. Defensive tackle

    c. Free safety

    d. Nose tackle

13. In 1989, Keith Millard was the NFL Defensive Player of the Year after recording 18 sacks from the middle of the Vikings' defense. Which USFL team did Minnesota pick him up from in 1985 before that league went bust?

    a. Arizona Outlaws

    b. Jacksonville Bulls

    c. Portland Breakers

    d. San Antonio Gunslingers

14. Todd Steussie was part of a huge offensive line for the Vikings from 1994 to 2000. How many playoff games did he play in, including the NFC Championship games in 1998 and 2000?

    a. 6
    b. 10
    c. 12
    d. 16

15. Jeff Christy bolstered both the Minnesota and Tampa Bay offensive lines during his career. Which of the following positions did Christy NOT play as a four-year starter and record-breaker at Freeport (PA) High?

    a. Fullback
    b. Linebacker
    c. Kicker
    d. Quarterback

16. When David Tukatahi Dixon broke into the NFL to block in 1992, he was only the second Maori (from New Zealand) ever to play in the league. Who was the first?

    a. Johan Asiata
    b. Riki Ellison
    c. Tevita Finau
    d. Will Hinchcliff

17. Randall McDaniel still holds the fastest-ever 100-yard dash time among offensive linemen in the NFL. What did he clock?

a. 9.95 seconds

b. seconds

c. seconds

d. seconds

18. Grady Alderman played in three Super Bowls and six Pro Bowls with Detroit and Minnesota from 1961 to 1974. He's also known as "the last of the original _____." What's missing?

a. Neanderthals

b. Nice guys

c. Tough guys

d. Vikings

19. Since 1987, former Minnesota lineman Tim Irwin has sponsored the Tim Irwin/Food City Bass Tournament held in Lenoir City, Tennessee. Proceeds from the tournament benefit the Boys & Girls Clubs of the Tennessee Valley, and over $1 million has been raised since 1990.

a. True

b. False

20. Which player did Minnesota trade away in 1968 to secure the services at guard of USC's All-American tackle Ron Yary?

a. Fred Cox

b. Carl Eller

c. Paul Krause

d. Fran Tarkenton

QUIZ ANSWERS

1. B – Hardware Hank

2. B – Gary Larsen

3. D – "Meet at the quarterback"

4. B – Most Valuable Player

5. C – 218

6. B – 11

7. C – 30

8. A – True

9. A – Concordia College

10. D – Williams Wrecking Crew

11. B – 22

12. A – Defensive end

13. B – Jacksonville Bulls

14. B – 10

15. D – Quarterback

16. B – Riki Ellison

17. C – 10.64 seconds

18. D – Vikings

19. A – True

20. D – Fran Tarkenton

DID YOU KNOW?

1. Jim Marshall revealed that the players disliked the name "Purple People Eaters" and called themselves "The Purple Gang" but added, "We've got to ride with it because it's our handle." The group was a major factor in the Vikings' postseason success from the late 1960s through the 1970s.

2. The Purple People Eaters were easily one of the most identifiable front fours in NFL history, along with the "Fearsome Foursome" of the Los Angeles Rams during the 1960s and early '70s, the "Steel Curtain" of the Pittsburgh Steelers during the '70s, the "New York Sack Exchange" of the New York Jets during the '80s, and the 1985 Chicago Bears' "Monsters of the Midway."

3. After each football season nowadays, the Carl Eller Award is given to the University of Minnesota's Defensive Player of the Year. Eller was elected to the College Football Hall of Fame in 2006.

4. Besides eating people, Jim Marshall is probably best known for his "wrong-way run," a play where he recovered a fumble and galloped 66 yards in the wrong direction into his own end zone and then threw the ball out of bounds, resulting in a safety for the San Francisco 49ers.

5. Defensive end John Randle was told by the Vikings that he would be signed as an undrafted free agent in 1990 only if he came back with his weight over 250 pounds. He actually weighed 244 pounds, so when he was put on the scale, he hid a chain and lock under his sweats to bring his weight up.

6. As a pro player, Korey Stringer was well liked inside the locker room and out. After a Vikings game, he stopped to help a fan change a flat tire and later signed over his Pro Bowl appearance check to a youth football program in his hometown of Warren, Ohio.

7. Randall McDaniel started every Vikings regular-season game from 1990 to 1999 and played in a record 11 straight Pro Bowls. He's widely recognized as one of the greatest and most versatile offensive linemen ever to play the game.

8. In 1990, Tim Irwin earned his law degree and was admitted to the Tennessee bar. In 2000, he opened his own law office in Knoxville, Tennessee, where he practiced in criminal defense, juvenile justice, personal injury, and sports law areas.

9. After left tackle Gary Zimmerman felt that a reporter distorted some of his postgame comments early in his career, he decided not to talk to the press at all. It was a practice he continued throughout his 13-year career.

10. Ron Yary gave due credit for his 2001 Pro Football Hall of Fame induction to his former coaches: John Ashton

(Bellflower High School in Los Angeles), John McKay (USC), and Bud Grant (Vikings). He also praised his position coaches: Marv Goux, Dave Levy, John Michaels, and Minnesota's Jerry Burns.

CHAPTER 7:

NO AIR ZONE

QUIZ TIME!

1. When Bobby Bryant started his Vikings career in 1968, he immediately teamed with Paul Krause to steal footballs from opponents for the next 12 seasons. How many interceptions did they combine for in that time?

    a. 82

    b. 93

    c. 104

    d. 121

2. Bryant had arguably his best game in the 1976 NFC Championship game with two picks off the Rams' Pat Haden and the return of a blocked Tom Dempsey field goal for a touchdown. How long was that return?

    a. 70 yards

    b. 80 yards

    c. 90 yards

    d. 94 yards

3. On March 5, 2004, the Minnesota Vikings signed cornerback Antoine Winfield Sr. to a six-year, $34.8 million contract as a free agent. How much was his signing bonus?

   a. $5.8 million
   b. $8.8 million
   c. $10.8 million
   d. $13.8 million

4. After 11 years with the Vikings, which included 31 interceptions, Carl Lee accepted a coaching offer at West Virginia State University in 1996 where he compiled a 34-75 record. What's the school's mascot?

   a. Bayou Wildcats
   b. Mountaineers
   c. Rattlesnakes
   d. Yellow Jackets

5. Cornerback Ed Sharockman was drafted by Minnesota with the 57th overall pick in the 1961 NFL Draft. He went on to play 11 solid seasons for the Vikes. Which AFL team also tried to secure his services?

   a. Dallas Texans
   b. Houston Oilers
   c. New York Titans
   d. Oakland Raiders

6. To this day, many fans and pundits believe that the Cowboys' Drew Pearson shoved Minnesota's Nate Wright on the game-winning Hail Mary, allowing Dallas

to win in the 1975 NFC Championship game. Who was the Cowboys' quarterback?

a. Troy Aikman
b. "Dandy" Don Meredith
c. Tony Romo
d. Roger Staubach

7. John Turner was part of several devastating pairings in the Minnesota defensive backfield. Which cornerback joined him in 1981?

a. Windlan Hall
b. Tommy Hannon
c. Willie Teal
d. Phil Wise

8. Issiac Holt played for Alcorn State, and is remembered for the game his senior year when he "held" future Hall-of-Famer Jerry Rice to 134 yards receiving. Which university did Rice play for in 1984?

a. Grambling State University
b. Howard University
c. Mississippi Valley State
d. University of Mississippi

9. Paul Krause is considered by many as the greatest "ball ____" in NFL history, picking off 53 passes with Minnesota and another 28 with Washington for an all-time record of 81. What's missing?

a. criminal
b. eagle

c. hawk

d. thief

10. In his first year in Minnesota (1968), Krause picked off passes in six straight games—still a team record. His total of 53 picks as a Viking is also a team mark. Finally, he holds the team record with 825 yards on interception returns.

   a. True

   b. False

11. Joey Browner was the USC Trojans' Most Valuable Player in 1982. Which other future Hall-of-Famer did he outplay for the award?

   a. Jeff Fisher

   b. Ty Law

   c. Ronnie Lott

   d. Deion Sanders

12. Robert Griffith was the Vikings' starting strong safety for six years. He was one of the NFL's most dreaded defenders. No receiver went over the middle against him and Minnesota without paying the "_____." What's the missing word?

   a. Bounty

   b. Price

   c. Surcharge

   d. Toll

13. Orlando Thomas played safety as a Viking for six seasons. He married his wife Demetra only two months after they first dated. Where did they meet in Minneapolis?

    a. Cheese Car Wash
    b. Cheesecake Factory
    c. Chuck E. Cheese Family Restaurant
    d. Murray's Cheese Bar

14. Harrison Smith received positive reviews in almost every scoring category at Notre Dame's Pro Day in 2012. What was the only aspect of his game that was negatively reviewed?

    a. Athletic ability
    b. Consistency
    c. Intelligence
    d. Man-to-man coverage ability

15. Cameron Dantzler picked off a pass by Louisville's Lamar Jackson (the Heisman Trophy winner) while he played for Mississippi State. What was the name of the 2017 bowl game the interception took place in?

    a. Gator Bowl
    b. Orange Bowl
    c. Rose Bowl
    d. TaxSlayer Bowl

16. Vikings cornerback Mike Hughes played on the University of Central Florida's undefeated national championship team in 2017. He returned a kickoff 95

yards for a decisive touchdown against the South Florida Bulls. What was that heated game called?

a. Florida Football Fest

b. Sunshine State Super Bowl

c. Tremor in Tampa

d. War on I-4

17. Cornerback Jeff Gladney was drafted by the Vikings as the 31st overall pick in the 2020 Draft. What were his first words to coach Mike Zimmer soon after his selection was announced?

a. "I've been waiting for you guys to call!"

b. "Now we can get down to business!"

c. "What took you characters so long?"

d. "You won't ever regret this!"

18. In the 2019 NFC Wild Card game against the New Orleans Saints, safety Anthony Harris intercepted a pass thrown by Drew Brees and ran it back 30 yards during the overtime win. What was the final score?

a. 21-17

b. 21-20

c. 24-21

d. 26-20

19. In 2014, Xavier Rhodes led the Vikings and finished fourth in the league in pass deflections. How many times did he tip the ball that year?

a. 6

b. 12

c. 18

d. 23

20. Captain Munnerlyn was born three months premature and grew up in Happy Hills, one of the toughest parts of Mobile, Alabama. He credits his mother's prayers for helping him make it to the NFL.

a. True

b. False

QUIZ ANSWERS

1. C – 104

2. C – 90 yards

3. C – $10.8 million

4. D – Yellow Jackets

5. A – Dallas Texans

6. D – Roger Staubach

7. C – Willie Teal

8. C – Mississippi Valley State

9. C – hawk

10. B – False (Krause holds the team record for interception returns with 852 yards.)

11. C – Ronnie Lott

12. B – Price

13. A – Cheese Car Wash

14. D – Man-to-man coverage ability

15. D – TaxSlayer Bowl

16. D – War on I-4

17. A – "I've been waiting for you guys to call!"

18. D – 26-20

19. C – 18

20. A – True

DID YOU KNOW?

1. Bobby Bryant would have a tough time making a roster today in the NFL. A 170 pound (77 kg) cornerback, he was never the fastest, strongest, or most intimidating player on the team. In street clothes, he looked more like a substitute teacher than an NFL star.

2. Many consider Antoine Winfield to be one of the best tacklers to play the cornerback position in the history of the pro game. In his nine years with the Vikings, Winfield crunched more than 700 tackles, despite missing time for injury on several occasions.

3. Ed Sharockman was the first cornerback ever selected by the Vikings in the draft. He lived up to that billing over his years with the team. A starter for 10 consecutive seasons from 1962 to 1971, he played on four division championship teams and was a starter in Super Bowl IV.

4. Nate Wright was pushed to the ground on the Hail Mary play against Dallas in the 1975 playoffs. The resulting Cowboys' touchdown knocked what might have been the best Vikings squad ever out of the playoffs, and framed Wright in history as "that guy that Drew Pearson shoved."

5. Known primarily as a terrific tackler, Joey Browner surprisingly snagged 37 interceptions, good for fourth on

the Vikings' all-time list. His 1,098 tackles is the fifth-highest total in team history.

6. After his playing days were done, Robert Griffith served as an executive member of the National Football League Players Association (NFLPA) for six years. He also became CEO and Chairman of Matador Enterprises and founder of the RG Foundation, giving college scholarships to high school students.

7. Sadly, Karl Kassulke is known for the tragic motorcycle accident he suffered on his way to training camp in 1973. It left him paralyzed from the waist down and ended a stellar career. Many fans don't realize that he played safety ferociously for 10 years before the accident.

8. Orlando Thomas intercepted nine passes in his 1995 rookie season—still a team record for rookies. As a result, he was selected for the Second Team All-NFC for his "picky" performance.

9. In 2017, Harrison Smith was rated the third-best player in the NFL by Pro Football Focus. His season score of 98.8 was also the highest among safeties in Pro Football Focus history. He was named to his third consecutive Pro Bowl on January 22, 2018.

10. In his 2018 NFL debut, Mike Hughes rocked a 28-yard interception return for a touchdown in the Vikings' 24-16 season-opening victory over the San Francisco 49ers.

CHAPTER 8:

SUPER BOWL SALUTE

QUIZ TIME!

1. The Vikings have come ever so close to hoisting the Lombardi Trophy given for winning the Super Bowl, but have always come up short. Which is the only other NFL team to make it to the big game four times and lose?

   a. Buffalo Bills
   b. Cincinnati Bengals
   c. Detroit Lions
   d. Houston Texans

2. In wet conditions, the Kansas City defense truly dominated Minnesota in Super Bowl IV. How many rushing yards did the Chiefs limit the Vikings to in that contest?

   a. 55
   b. 67
   c. 89
   d. 95

3. The Vikings, led by head coach Bud Grant, entered the 1970 Super Bowl with an NFL-best 12-2 regular-season record. They led the "older" league in total points scored (379) and fewest points allowed (133), and they'd racked up 50 or more points in three different games.

   a. True
   b. False

4. On January 13, 1974, the Vikings played in the second Super Bowl in franchise history against the Miami Dolphins. Where was the game played?

   a. Houston, Texas
   b. Los Angeles, California
   c. Miami, Florida
   d. Phoenix, Arizona

5. Super Bowl VIII, in which Minnesota played against the Dolphins in 1974, was the last ever to feature a peculiar aspect of traditional football fields. What was it?

   a. Fields that were 110 yards long
   b. Fields without any covered benches
   c. Goalposts at the front of the end zone
   d. Goalposts without protective padding

6. Minnesota's best chance to challenge Miami in Super Bowl VIII occurred with less than a minute remaining in the first half, but a Vikings running back fumbled the ball away at the Dolphins' 6-yard line. After that, the Vikes were unable to overcome Miami's lead in the second half. Who was the culprit?

a. Chuck Foreman

b. Tommy Mason

c. Oscar Reed

d. Rickey Young

7. While Minnesota had the monstrous "Purple People Eaters" on the defensive side of the ball, what was the nickname of the vaunted Miami defense in 1974 featuring Nick Buoniconti, Dick Anderson, and Jake Scott?

a. Bay of Biscayne Brawlers

b. Miami Mashers

c. No Name Defense

d. South Florida Squashers

8. The number of passes attempted by Miami quarterback Bob Griese in Super Bowl VIII was also a record low. How many times did Bob dare to air it out against the Vikes?

a. 5

b. 7

c. 10

d. 13

9. Tarkenton set what was then a record for completions by a quarterback in the NFL's biggest game. How many passes did Fran complete in the 1974 game?

a. 18

b. 25

c. 30

d. 34

10. Besides announcers Ray Scott and Pat Summerall, which former star player graced the broadcast booth while adding color commentary to the 1974 Super Bowl?

    a. Terry Bradshaw

    b. Jim Brown

    c. O.J. Simpson

    d. Bart Starr

11. What was the cost of a 30-second commercial on the CBS network during Super Bowl VIII?

    a. $55,000

    b. $103,000

    c. $224,000

    d. $353,000

12. When the Vikings appeared in the Super Bowl again in 1975, they faced a stingy Steelers defense. What was that group's apt nickname?

    a. Pittsburgh Pride

    b. The Baddest of the Burgh

    c. The Steel Curtain

    d. The Steel Wall

13. How many fans packed the Tulane Stadium in New Orleans to witness the 16-6 Steelers victory over the Vikings that year?

    a. 66,556

    b. 74,447

    c. 80,997

    d. 92,119

14. Minnesota was in the Super Bowl in 1975 because their defense had again saved the day in the NFC Championship game, stopping their opponents cold on their own 2-yard line. Who was the unlucky foe?

    a. Dallas Cowboys
    b. Green Bay Packers
    c. Los Angeles Rams
    d. St. Louis Cardinals

15. Entering Super Bowl IX, the Vikings looked to redeem themselves after a one-sided Bowl loss the previous year, making it their second Bowl defeat. They had just won the NFC Central for the sixth time in seven seasons.

    a. True
    b. False

16. Who was the only Minnesota Viking in history to both punt and pass in the Super Bowl?

    a. Neil Clabo
    b. Greg Coleman
    c. Bob Lee
    d. Harry Newsome

17. Which member of the 1973 Vikings already possessed two Super Bowl rings when he took the field for the Bowl in Houston?

    a. Carroll Dale
    b. Carl Eller
    c. Ed Marinaro
    d. Brent McClanahan

18. In Super Bowl XI, the Vikings again had a powerful offense led by 39-year-old quarterback Fran Tarkenton and running back Chuck Foreman. In his 16th NFL season, Tarkenton was already the league's all-time leader in pass completions (3,186), passing yards (41,802), and touchdown passes (308).

    a. True
    b. False

19. Which future Viking, at that time playing for the Oakland Raiders, scored the first touchdown against Minnesota in Super Bowl XI?

    a. George Blanda
    b. Dave Casper
    c. Kenny Stabler
    d. Gene Upshaw

20. After all was said and done, Minnesota great Fran Tarkenton said, "If football taught me anything about _____, it is that you win the game one play at a time." What's missing?

    a. business
    b. disappointment
    c. life
    d. winning

QUIZ ANSWERS

1. A – Buffalo Bills

2. B – 67

3. A – True

4. A – Houston, Texas

5. C – Goalposts at the front of the end zone

6. C – Oscar Reed

7. C – No Name Defense

8. B – 7

9. A – 18

10. D – Bart Starr

11. B – $103,000

12. C – The Steel Curtain

13. C – 80,997

14. C – Los Angeles Rams

15. A – True

16. C – Bob Lee

17. A – Carroll Dale

18. B – False (In Super Bowl XI, Tarkenton was 36 years old, not 39.)

19. B – Dave Casper

20. A – business

DID YOU KNOW?

1. Even though the upstart New York Jets from the AFL had won the previous Super Bowl, many pundits continued to believe the NFL was still superior to the AFL. Thus, they fully expected the Vikings to defeat the Kansas City Chiefs in 1970, and Minnesota entered the Super Bowl as 12.5- to 13.5-point favorites.

2. By winning the NFL championship in 1969, the Vikings became the last holders of the Ed Thorp Memorial Trophy given to the champions of the NFL beginning in 1934. The trophy was named after Ed Thorp, a noted referee, rules expert, sporting goods dealer, and friend of many early NFL owners.

3. In the 1970 Bowl, Bud Grant bucked tradition by becoming the first Super Bowl coach not to wear a tie. His counterpart, Hank Stram, wore a three-piece suit, with a red vest and a blazer with the Chiefs' helmet logo neatly stitched on the breast pocket.

4. The Super Bowl back in the day featured a vastly different type of halftime show than nowadays. The halftime entertainment during Super Bowl VIII was provided by the University of Texas Longhorn Band and the Westchester Wranglerettes.

5. In the 1974 Super Bowl affair, Miami's Jim Langer explained why his team was perhaps a step ahead of the

Minnesota gang: "We just hit the Vikings defense so hard and so fast that they didn't know what hit them. Alan Page later said he knew we would dominate them after only the first couple of plays."

6. In 1975, the Steelers limited the Vikings to Super Bowl record lows of nine first downs, 119 total offensive yards, 17 rushing yards, and no offensive scores. Minnesota's only points came on a blocked punt, and they couldn't even convert the extra point attempt.

7. In Super Bowl IX, Pittsburgh running back Franco Harris ran for a Super Bowl record 158 yards (more than the entire Minnesota offense) and a touchdown. He was named the game's Most Valuable Player.

8. The Vikings were designated the "home" team in the 1975 Bowl. They had worn their purple jerseys at home anyway for much of their history, aside from a few games in the 1960s, when the NFL was encouraging (but not requiring) teams to wear white at home.

9. The Vikings became the first team ever to appear in four Super Bowls in 1977, a record they held until the Dallas Cowboys made it to a Super Bowl for the fifth time in Super Bowl XIII.

10. In their four Super Bowls, the Vikings never led once, so viewers never saw what the Vikings could do with a lead in a Super Bowl game. Minnesota also was never able to score any points in the first half. Turnovers prevented the club from a likely score on three occasions.

CHAPTER 9:

SHINING THE BUSTS

QUIZ TIME!

1. Besides running back Hugh McElhenny, who was the other Viking to first play in the Pro Bowl in 1962?

   a. Grady Alderman

   b. Jerry Huth

   c. Jerry Reichow

   d. Mick Tingelhoff

2. Tommy Mason became the first Minnesota player to be named All-Pro in 1963. How many yards did he gain that year?

   a. 672

   b. 763

   c. 888

   d. 1,015

3. Alan Page was named both the AP NFL Defensive Player of the Year and the MVP in 1971. Who's the only other defensive player ever to win the MVP?

a. Dick Butkus

b. Ray Lewis

c. Lawrence Taylor

d. Reggie White

4. Purple People Eaters Carl Eller and Alan Page were eventually inducted into the Pro Football Hall of Fame. Many fans, players, coaches, and sportswriters argue that Jim Marshall should be a Hall-of-Famer as well.

a. True

b. False

5. In franchise history, the Vikings have retired six uniform numbers. Which of the following players is NOT among them?

a. Cris Carter (#80)

b. Joe Kapp (#22)

c. Korey Stringer (#77)

d. Fran Tarkenton (#10)

6. In 1972, a Minnesota executive made a daring trade with the New York Giants, bringing Fran Tarkenton back to the Vikings. Who was this manager, who was later elected to the Hall of Fame?

a. Lester Bagley

b. Don Becker

c. Jim Finks

d. Rick Spielman

7. Besides Marv Levy, Bud Grant is the only coach in history to take teams to both the Grey Cup in Canada and the Super Bowl. In what year was he inducted into the Hall of Fame?

   a. 1984
   b. 1988
   c. 1994
   d. 1999

8. Fran Tarkenton won the NFL Most Valuable Player award in 1975. What other prestigious award did he receive the same year?

   a. Bert Bell Award
   b. Comeback Player of the Year
   c. Heisman Trophy
   d. Rookie of the Year

9. When Adrian Peterson won the MVP in 2012, which other rapid running back did he tie for the eighth-highest number of all-purpose yards from scrimmage (2,314) in a single season?

   a. Marcus Allen
   b. Eric Dickerson
   c. Edgerrin James
   d. Gale Sayers

10. Peterson was named to the NFL 2010s All-Decade Team. Which of the following players was NOT named to the same squad?

a. Tom Brady

b. Frank Gore

c. Larry Fitzgerald

d. Matthew Stafford

11. Out of Nebraska, Mick Tingelhoff was the ultimate award-winning center for the Vikings. Which of the following awards did he NOT win?

a. Nebraska Hall of Fame inductee

b. Offensive Player of the Year

c. Seven-time All-NFL Center

d. Six NFL Pro Bowls

12. Matt Birk was another outstanding Minnesota center. With which team did he cop a Super Bowl ring?

a. Baltimore Ravens

b. Denver Broncos

c. New England Patriots

d. Philadelphia Eagles

13. This fearsome Minnesota linebacker is a member of the Vikings' Ring of Honor. He also served as the face of the Multiple Sclerosis "Read-a-Thon" for many years. Who was he?

a. Matt Blair

b. Chad Greenway

c. E.J. Henderson

d. Jeff Siemon

14. Gary Zimmerman is considered one of the best ever at protecting Minnesota quarterbacks. He's also one of the few players in league history to be named to two All-Decade Teams: the 1980s and '90s. What was his uniform number?

    a. 59
    b. 65
    c. 68
    d. 73

15. Joey Browner is still remembered as one of the hardest-hitting safeties in NFL lore. How many times did he make the "All-Madden Team" (named after famous coach John Madden)?

    a. 4
    b. 6
    c. 7
    d. 9

16. During his relatively short stint with the Vikings, Keith Millard had 53 sacks and recovered seven fumbles. When did he win the AP Defensive Player of the Year Award?

    a. 1979
    b. 1895
    c. 1989
    d. 1994

17. This player is still the all-time Vikings scoring leader. He was selected for the Pro Bowl in 1970. Who is he?

a. Cris Carter

b. Fred Cox

c. Ryan Longwell

d. Adrian Peterson

18. Defensive end Jared Allen holds the Minnesota single-season sack record with how many?

   a. 14

   b. 19

   c. 22

   d. 28

19. Cris Carter boasts the following distinctions: Eight-time Pro-Bowler; two-time First Team All-Pro; Vikings career leader in receptions, receiving yards, and receiving touchdowns; Hall of Fame (2013) inductee.

   a. True

   b. False

20. "His stance was awful, and his technique was even worse, but he kept defenders out of the Minnesota backfield. He was a gifted athlete, able to dunk a basketball from a flatfooted start." Who was this character, also elected to the Hall of Fame in 2009?

   a. David Dixon

   b. Steve Hutchinson

   c. Randall McDaniel

   d. Milt Sunde

QUIZ ANSWERS

1. C – Jerry Reichow

2. B – 763

3. C – Lawrence Taylor

4. A – True

5. B – Joe Kapp (#22)

6. C – Jim Finks

7. C – 1994

8. A – Bert Bell Award

9. A – Marcus Allen

10. D – Matthew Stafford

11. B – Offensive Player of the Year

12. A – Baltimore Ravens

13. A – Matt Blair

14. B – 65

15. A – 4

16. C – 1989

17. B – Fred Cox

18. C – 22

19. A – True

20. C – Randall McDaniel

DID YOU KNOW?

1. The 1969 NFL Championship Game was the 37th and final championship game before the AFL-NFL merger. It was played on January 4, 1970, at Metropolitan Stadium in Bloomington, Minnesota, a suburb south of Minneapolis. The Vikings crushed Cleveland, 27-7.

2. Alan Page wasn't just the first defensive player ever to win the MVP award in the NFL. In 1992, Page was elected to an open seat as an Associate Justice of the Minnesota Supreme Court, becoming the first African-American to serve on that court.

3. From 1968, the so-called "Purple People Eaters" were a key part of a Vikings team that won 10 division titles in 11 years, leading to five NFC Championships and four Super Bowl appearances.

4. Speaking of accolades, Eller, Larsen, Page, and Marshall were chosen for the Vikings' 25th Anniversary team, while Eller, Page, and Marshall were selected to the Vikings' 40th Anniversary team. Finally, Eller, Larsen, Page, Marshall, and Sutherland were selected to join the 50 Greatest Vikings.

5. Before coaching Minnesota, Bud Grant played for the Minneapolis Lakers of the NBA, the Philadelphia Eagles of the NFL, and the Winnipeg Blue Bombers of the CFL. A

statue of Grant proudly stands in front of the Winnipeg Blue Bombers' current stadium, IG Field.

6. At the time of his retirement in 1979, Fran Tarkenton owned every major quarterback record. He was inducted into the Pro Football Hall of Fame in 1986 and the College Football Hall of Fame in 1987.

7. Few defensive ends ever had Chris Doleman's combination of speed, strength, and athleticism. He tallied 31 of his 44 forced fumbles and 96.5 of his 150.5 sacks (fourth in NFL history) with the Vikings. Chris was elected to the Hall of Fame in 2012.

8. At Oregon, Ahmad Rashād, then known as Bobby Moore, played wide receiver and wingback as a sophomore in 1969, making the all-conference team. He switched to running back, where he was an All-American in 1971 in the same backfield with quarterback Dan Fouts. Rashād was named to the College Football Hall of Fame on May 9, 2007.

9. Paul Krause was way ahead of his time, playing the safety position like a cornerback. While the defensive line got most of the credit, Krause was the true heart of the great Minnesota defenses of the 1970s. He was elected to the Hall of Fame in 1998.

10. John Randle had a motor that simply wouldn't quit. The former Vikings' standout is one of the few undrafted free agents ever to be elected to the Pro Football Hall of Fame, and his record of eight straight double-digit sack seasons by a defensive tackle may never be matched.

CHAPTER 10:

DRAFT DAY

QUIZ TIME!

1. This player was drafted in the 1st round with the 19th overall pick by the Vikings in 1983. He led Minnesota in nine different statistical categories during his career. Who was this hit man?

    a. Joey Browner
    b. Robert Griffith
    c. Antoine Winfield
    d. Roy Winston

2. Drafted by the Vikes in 1974, Matt Blair quickly established himself as one of the speediest linebackers in the NFC, earning Pro Bowl honors in six consecutive seasons (1977-82), and making the NFL All-Rookie Team. Where was he born?

    a. Cincinnati, Ohio
    b. Dayton, Ohio
    c. Hilo, Hawaii
    d. Stillwater, Oklahoma

3. Robert Smith was drafted by the Vikings in the 1st round of the 1993 NFL Draft with the 21st overall pick. He still holds the league record for average yards per touchdown run at 31.2.

   a. True
   b. False

4. Matt Birk is probably the biggest "_____" in the Vikings' draft history. With their 6th round pick in the 1998 NFL Draft, Minnesota selected the 6'4", 300-pound center out of Harvard. What's missing?

   a. bargain
   b. dud
   c. steal
   d. washout

5. Adrian Peterson "fell into the Vikings' lap" as the 7th overall pick in the 2007 Draft. What previous injury in college allowed him to stay available so long?

   a. Ankle
   b. Collarbone
   c. Knee
   d. Shoulder

6. Before the 1998 NFL Draft, one dynamic player vowed that teams that passed on him "will regret it once they see what kind of a player I am and what kind of guy I really am." Who was this character?

   a. Cris Carter
   b. Percy Harvin

c. Randy Moss

d. Ahmad Rashād

7. After a sterling USC career, Ron Yary was chosen by the Vikings as the 1st overall pick in the 1968 NFL Draft. Yary became the first offensive lineman selected with the top pick in draft history. It took another 29 years to happen again, when Orlando Pace was picked by St. Louis.

a. True

b. False

8. Chris Doleman was drafted by the Vikings in 1985 as an outside linebacker. What position did the team move him to that allowed his natural tackling talent to flourish?

a. Cornerback

b. Defensive end

c. Nickelback

d. Safety

9. Drafted in 1967, this Viking took up long-distance running in the middle of his football career, and his weight dropped below 220 pounds (100 kg). Yet he was still a sack master. Who was he?

a. Carl Eller

b. Gary Larsen

c. Jim Marshall

d. Alan Page

10. Minnesota drafted Fran Tarkenton in the 3rd round out of Georgia in 1961. "I _____ because I'm good at it, and we

get a lot of touchdowns that way," he said confidently. What's missing?

a. dodge
b. pass
c. run
d. scramble

11. Minnesota has had a few draft busts, like Tyrell Johnson, the 43rd pick in 2008. How many tackles was Johnson responsible for in four years?

a. 110
b. 123
c. 145
d. 177

12. Which player did Minnesota trade "back" in the 2005 Draft, thinking they had found their franchise quarterback?

a. Kerry Collins
b. Carson Palmer
c. Tarvaris Jackson
d. Steve McNair

13. After being drafted in 1987, D.J. Dozier's best season in Minnesota was his rookie season: 257 yards rushing, five rushing touchdowns, two receiving touchdowns, and 89 receiving yards. From there, it went downhill. In four years as a Viking, he gained just 643 yards.

a. True
b. False

14. When Minnesota drafted Darrin Nelson with the 7ᵗʰ pick in the 1982 Draft, which future superstar did they miss out on three picks later?

    a. Marcus Allen
    b. Tony Dorsett
    c. Walter Payton
    d. Curt Warner

15. When the Vikings traded future Hall-of-Famer Randy Moss to Oakland in 2007, which receiver did they select with one of the picks they got in return?

    a. Tony Gonzalez
    b. Derrick Mason
    c. Wes Welker
    d. Troy Williamson

16. In six seasons, the 2ⁿᵈ pick in 1967 didn't ever post a double-digit season in rushing touchdowns and failed ever to rush for more than 700 yards in a 14-game season. Who was he?

    a. Bill Brown
    b. Earl Denny
    c. Clinton Jones
    d. Jim Lindsey

17. Defensive end Dimitrius Underwood was drafted by Minnesota as the 29ᵗʰ pick in the 1999 Draft. Yet he never played a down with the Vikings. What happened?

    a. He decided to become a minister.

b. He walked off the field in training camp and never returned.

c. He was badly injured and never played pro football.

d. The draft pick was rescinded by the NFL.

18. When he first took over as general manager of the Vikings, which player did Rick Spielman draft along with Adrian Peterson in 2007?

   a. Anthony Barr

   b. Matt Kalil

   c. Cordarrelle Patterson

   d. Sidney Rice

19. Before 2021, Spielman shared a "triangle of authority" in drafts with Vikings owner Zygi Wilf and the Minnesota coach at the time. Who was the latter?

   a. Brad Childress

   b. Bud Grant

   c. Dennis Green

   d. Mike Tice

20. Which star wide receiver was drafted in 2014 who went on to lead the Minnesota team in receiving yards with 720?

   a. Joe Banyard

   b. Stefon Diggs

   c. Christian Ponder

   d. Ben Tate

QUIZ ANSWERS

1. A – Joey Browner

2. C – Hilo, Hawaii

3. B – False (Robert Smith's NFL record is 27.2, not 31.2, yards averaged on his touchdown runs.)

4. C – steal

5. B – Collarbone

6. C – Randy Moss

7. A – True

8. B – Defensive end

9. D – Alan Page

10. D – scramble

11. B – 123

12. C – Tarvaris Jackson

13. A – True

14. A – Marcus Allen

15. D – Troy Williamson

16. C – Clinton Jones

17. B – He walked off the field in training camp and never returned.

18. D – Sidney Rice

19. A – Brad Childress

20. B – Stefon Diggs

DID YOU KNOW?

1. On December 27, 1960, Tulane running back Tommy Mason was taken with the 1st overall choice and the first-ever draft pick used by the Vikings. Also chosen that year were quarterback Fran Tarkenton (in the 3rd round) and defensive back Ed Sharockman (5th round).

2. Chuck Foreman was sitting in his University of Miami apartment in 1973 when he learned that he had been drafted. At first, he felt consternation about playing in Minnesota due to the cold, recollecting a time when flamethrowers were used to thaw the Metropolitan Stadium field before a game.

3. As a 1st round pick (9th overall) in the 2003 Draft, Kevin Williams became a starter for the Vikings on day one of his NFL career. As a rookie, he had 37 tackles and 10.5 sacks.

4. When he was drafted in 1964, most Minnesota fans already knew Carl Eller from his play on the University of Minnesota football team. He helped lead the Golden Gophers to a Big Ten Conference Championship and National Championship in the 1960 season. He was also a two-time All-American.

5. During the 1998 NFL Draft, Randy Moss was projected as a high first-round pick but was taken by the Minnesota Vikings with the 21st overall pick after a number of NFL

teams—even those in need of a wide receiver—worried about Moss's well-documented legal problems.

6. After his first season, Randall McDaniel went on to become one of the most dominating left guards ever to play the sport. Drafted in 1988, he was selected to an NFL-record 12 consecutive Pro Bowls from 1989 to 2000.

7. The year 2005 was a terrible draft year for Minnesota. With two 1st round picks, Minnesota selected two players (including Erasmus James) who were no longer in the NFL just five years later.

8. Instead of drafting Warren Sapp (who went on to torment the Vikings with Tampa Bay), Minnesota chose defensive end Derrick Alexander, who spent four seasons in Minneapolis and never reached double-digit sacks—a must for a defensive end taken in the 1st round.

9. Before the "disastrous" drafting of quarterback Tarvaris Jackson in 2005, SI.com had assessed him this way: "A developmental prospect who could be stashed on a practice squad, Jackson still needs a season or two to complete his game."

10. The Gerald Robinson era in Minnesota isn't necessarily defined as long or special. The defensive end, who was drafted out of Auburn, appeared in 16 games over two seasons and recorded one tackle, in 1987.

CHAPTER 11:

LET'S MAKE A DEAL

QUIZ TIME!

1. When Fran Tarkenton was traded to the Giants in 1967, the Vikings used one of the picks they acquired to sign a receiver who played in Minnesota for five seasons, putting up solid numbers. Who was he?

    a. Pat Flatley

    b. Bob Grim

    c. Marlin McKeever

    d. Gene Washington

2. The first time Tarkenton was traded away, the New York Giants were in desperate need of a talented quarterback. One reason for shipping Fran out was possible friction with his coach over differing styles of play. Who was the head man at the time?

    a. Jerry Burns

    b. Leslie Frazier

    c. Norm Van Brocklin

    d. Mike Zimmer

3. Warren Moon was dealt to the Vikings in 1994 at age 38 for two 4th round picks. Which team unloaded Warren?

    a. Chicago Bears

    b. Houston Oilers

    c. Jacksonville Jaguars

    d. Seattle Seahawks

4. Just before the 2008 Draft, the Vikings pulled off a blockbuster trade, scoring the marauding Jared Allen in the deal. What team did the Vikes pry him away from?

    a. Indianapolis Colts

    b. Kansas City Chiefs

    c. New York Jets

    d. San Diego Chargers

5. When the Vikings picked Danielle Hunter in the 2015 Draft, the selection had been traded to Minnesota by a nearby rival. Which team offloaded the pick?

    a. Cleveland Browns

    b. Detroit Lions

    c. Green Bay Packers

    d. Tennessee Titans

6. Bud Grant was able to organize an indirect trade for quarterback Joe Kapp, who effectively crossed the border from the British Columbia Lions. Who was the player the Vikings sent back to his home country of Canada?

    a. Jim Finks

    b. Wayne Gretzky

c. Max Winter

d. Jim Young

7. In 2004, Randy Moss was sidelined a bunch by a knee injury. Then on- and off-field antics finally led to his trade to Oakland. Who did the Vikings get in return?

a. Justin Fargas

b. Napoleon Harris

c. Heath Shuler

d. Troy Williamson

8. Minnesota originally believed they got the better end of the Herschel Walker deal. Instead, the Cowboys used the draft picks acquired in the trade to get the players needed to help win three Super Bowls in the 1990s. Meanwhile, the Vikings did not make a single Super Bowl appearance with Walker.

a. True

b. False

9. When new Dallas head coach Jimmy Johnson contacted Minnesota GM Mike Lynn about the possible deal, Lynn faxed back his interest immediately. How much did Dallas pay Walker as an "exit bonus"?

a. $500,000

b. $750,000

c. $1.25 million

d. $2.5 million

10. One "piece" in the original trade, Minnesota's Darrin Nelson, refused to report to Dallas and was then sent

packing to San Diego. How did Darrin find out he had been traded?

   a. From his agent

   b. From his wife

   c. On TV

   d. On the radio while in his car

11. How many seasons did Herschel Walker play for the Vikings following the trade?

   a. 1

   b. 2

   c. 4

   d. 6

12. When Minnesota quarterback Teddy Bridgewater went down with a serious knee injury just before the 2016 season, the Vikings' brass were able to trade for Sam Bradford. Which team gave him up?

   a. Atlanta Falcons

   b. Baltimore Ravens

   c. Las Vegas Raiders

   d. Philadelphia Eagles

13. Bradford won only three of his last 11 starts as a Viking. What nickname did he receive after reducing his passes to less than seven yards per attempt?

   a. Captain Checkdown

   b. Captain Courageous

   c. Sam "Short Pass" Bradford

   d. Sam "Short Sell" Bradford

14. Ultimately, Bradford's knee problems opened the door for another Minnesota quarterback who was responsible for the 2017 "Minneapolis Miracle" after which he led Vikings fans in the "Skol" chant. Who was he?

    a. Nick Foles
    b. Shaun Hill
    c. Brad Johnson
    d. Case Keenum

15. Executive Chris Spielman once said that you can use free agents to fill in roster gaps, but teams normally build with the draft. According to him, "You can't buy a _____." What's missing?

    a. Backfield
    b. Complete set of players
    c. Locker room
    d. Sky full of stars

16. One quarterback was traded by the Texans to the Vikings in 2009, and he thought he "was finally getting a chance to be the man." But then Minnesota wooed Brett Favre out of retirement. Who was the former?

    a. John David Booty
    b. Tarvaris Jackson
    c. Brady Quinn
    d. Sage Rosenfels

17. Vikings receiver Stefon Diggs was traded to the Buffalo Bills right before the 2020 season. How much was he scheduled to make that year?

a. $6.5 million

b. $8.2 million

c. $10.4 million

d. $11.5 million

18. What inspired the trade rumors swirling around Diggs late in his Vikings career?

    a. His family's unhappiness in Minneapolis

    b. His refusal to run certain pass routes

    c. Missed meetings and practices

    d. Multiple injuries

19. In 2019, Minnesota's Peter King even floated "him" as a potential trade chip if Minnesota were to hypothetically pursue a blockbuster Deshaun Watson swap. Who is "him"?

    a. Mike Boone

    b. Dalvin Cook

    c. Myles Gaskin

    d. Alexander Mattison

20. Rick Spielman was "at it again" when he engineered a rare intra-divisional trade with a rival during the 2020 NFL Draft. Which enemy was willing to deal?

    a. Chicago Bears

    b. Detroit Lions

    c. Green Bay Packers

    d. Tampa Bay Buccaneers

QUIZ ANSWERS

1. B – Bob Grim

2. C – Norm Van Brocklin

3. B – Houston Oilers

4. B – Kansas City Chiefs

5. B – Detroit Lions

6. D – Jim Young

7. B – Napoleon Harris

8. A – True

9. C – $1.25 million

10. D – On the radio while in his car

11. B – 2

12. D – Philadelphia Eagles

13. A – Captain Checkdown

14. D – Case Keenum

15. C – Locker room

16. D – Sage Rosenfels

17. D – $11.5 million

18. C – Missed meetings and practices

19. D – Alexander Mattison

20. A – Chicago Bears

DID YOU KNOW?

1. Fran Tarkenton was traded away and then traded for again by Minnesota. His second spell in Minnesota was better than his first—he played seven more years, went 64-27-2 as a starter, and never compiled a losing record. The Vikings won 10 or more games in three of those seasons, making five playoff appearances, and playing in three consecutive Super Bowls.

2. For two fourth-round draft picks, Warren Moon delivered one of the finest seasons of his career in 1995. The Vikings finished only 8-8, but that wasn't any fault of Moon's. He threw for 4,228 yards, 33 touchdowns, and 14 interceptions.

3. After they secured Jared Allen in a trade from the Chiefs in 2008, Minnesota promptly signed him to a six-year contract for over $73 million, making him the highest-paid defender in NFL history. Allen earned every penny of the deal, registering 85.5 sacks in 96 games and missing zero games.

4. What made the Allen deal even better for Minnesota was that the sixth-round pick they got turned out to be center John Sullivan, who had a long stretch as one of the NFL's better interior linemen before retiring in 2019.

5. Before the 1967 CFL season, Joe Kapp decided to return to the U.S. to play pro football. The AFL's Oakland Raiders,

San Diego Chargers, and Houston Oilers were hot in pursuit of him. But Minnesota got their man.

6. In 2021, rumors have it that the Vikings won't trade Kirk Cousins because head coach Mike Zimmer knows "he's another non-deep playoff run away from the unemployment line."

7. The 1989 Herschel Walker trade was the largest player trade in the history of the National Football League. Including Walker himself, the trade involved the San Diego Chargers, Dallas Cowboys, and Minnesota and eventually resulted in moving 18 players and draft picks.

8. Darrin Nelson went to Dallas after the trade and negotiated his re-trade to San Diego. He said, "If I were younger, I'd love to stay there. If I couldn't play for a contender, I told them I at least wanted to go to California or I would retire. You don't have much control in this business. You can't have a say unless you're older and don't have to play."

9. Just to highlight the complexity of the trade market: Due to conditions in the Walker deal, the Chargers sent a fifth-round pick in 1990 to the Vikings, who then shipped their sixth-round pick in '90 to the Cowboys, who also kept a second-round pick in 1991 from the Vikings as part of the original deal for Nelson.

10. The Vikings originally assumed they got the better end of the deal, not knowing at the time that Dallas coach Jimmy Johnson was mainly interested in the draft picks, not the

players. At a press conference after the trade, Johnson boasted that he'd committed "The Great Train Robbery."

CHAPTER 12:

WRITING THE RECORD BOOK

QUIZ TIME!

1. The Vikings have a better record against one nearby team (considering more than 25 games played against the opponent) than all others—namely the Detroit Lions. What's Minnesota's approximate winning percentage in this series?

   a. .553
   b. .664
   c. .688
   d. .725

2. The largest Minnesota margin of victory ever (48 points) came against the Cleveland Browns in 1969. What was the final score of that contest?

   a. 48-0
   b. 51-3
   c. 54-6
   d. 66-14

3. In which season did the Vikings win their most games ever (15)?

    a. 1974
    b. 1988
    c. 1998
    d. 2012

4. From 1974 to 1976, the Vikings steamrolled all opponents at home. How many consecutive games did they win in their cozy Minneapolis confines?

    a. 13
    b. 15
    c. 19
    d. 25

5. Only 11 Vikings have scored on punt returns, and Marcus Sherels leads Minnesota with five in his career. He also leads the team in punt returns with 231, and in return yardage with 2,447 yards. With a touchdown every 46 punt returns, Sherels was a special teams ace for the Vikings.

    a. True
    b. False

6. Cordarrelle Patterson recorded the longest-ever kickoff return for a touchdown in Minnesota history. How many yards did he scamper?

    a. 99
    b. 101
    c. 105
    d. 109

7. Although John Randle holds the career sacks record as a Viking, Carl Eller, Jim Marshall, and especially Alan Page aren't ranked because sacks were only noted after the Purple People Eaters had hung up their cleats. When were sacks first tallied?

   a. 1976
   b. 1980
   c. 1982
   d. 1988

8. Receiver Adam Thielen has an outside chance of catching enough passes to sneak up on all-time leader Cris Carter with 12,383 yards in the air. How many yards does Thielen have currently?

   a. 3,255
   b. 3,897
   c. 4,567
   d. 5,778

9. Even though Paul Krause holds the Vikings' record for interceptions with 53, another player more recently set the record for most career picks returned for touchdowns with four. Who was he?

   a. Bobby Bryant
   b. Carl Lee
   c. Harrison Smith
   d. Nate Wright

10. Fred Cox booted 1,365 points in his 15 seasons as a Viking. In how many seasons did he lead the NFL in made field goals?

a. 2

b. 3

c. 4

d. 6

11. A traditional straight-on style kicker, there's no way by today's standards that Cox's career would last half as long because he converted only __ percent of this field goal attempts. What percent?

a. 55

b. 62

c. 68

d. 78

12. A rapid return man from Los Alamitos, California, set the Vikings rookie record for punt return yards, with 247 — though he lasted only three NFL seasons. Who was he?

a. Keenan Howry

b. Bisi Johnson

c. K.J. Osborn

d. Marcus Sherels

13. Anthony Harris tied for the NFL lead with six interceptions in 2019, but the Vikings rookie record for picks in a season was nine. Who established that lofty mark in 1995?

a. Cameron Dantzler

b. Jeff Gladney

c. Keith Millard

d. Orlando Thomas

14. Brett Favre is the NFL's all-time leader in completions, attempts, yards, and touchdowns. He also holds a dubious record for throwing more interceptions than anyone else in league history. How many more than the next "worst"?

   a. 39
   b. 48
   c. 59
   d. 68

15. All three of the Vikings' single-season rookie receiving records belong to Randy Moss, who exploded on the scene in 1998 with 69 catches, 1,313 yards, and 17 touchdowns. A modern-day receiver could conceivably average 4.4 passes per game to hit 70 on the season (a record since broken by Justin Jefferson with 88 in 2020).

   a. True
   b. False

16. The largest home crowd ever to witness a Vikings game in 2019 was 67,157. Who was the worthy opponent?

   a. Chicago Bears
   b. Green Bay Packers
   c. Indianapolis Colts
   d. New England Patriots

17. In 2002, which fleet-footed runner scored a touchdown in seven consecutive games, a franchise record at the time?

   a. Matt Asiata
   b. Dalvin Cook

c. D.J. Dozier

d. Moe Williams

18. Gus Frerotte tossed the longest pass completion in Vikings' history with a 99-yarder to Bernard Berrian. What year was it?

a. 1897

b. 1999

c. 2008

d. 2013

19. When Adrian Peterson ran for 2,097 rushing yards in 2012, how many more yards did he need to break one of the most invincible records for single-season rushing set by Eric Dickerson?

a. 20

b. 15

c. 9

d. 5

20. The value of the Minnesota franchise, according to *Forbes* magazine in September 2020, was $2.95 billion. What was the price paid for the franchise back in 2005?

a. $885 million

b. $720 million

c. $600 million

d. $455 million

QUIZ ANSWERS

1. B – .664

2. B – 51-3

3. C – 1998

4. B – 15

5. A – True

6. D – 109

7. C – 1982

8. B – 3,897

9. C – Harrison Smith

10. B – 3

11. B – 62

12. A – Keenan Howry

13. D – Orlando Thomas

14. C – 59

15. A – True

16. B – Green Bay Packers

17. D – Moe Williams

18. C – 2008

19. C – 9

20. C – $600 million

DID YOU KNOW?

1. If head coach Mike Zimmer wants to reach the 158 wins that franchise leader Bud Grant piled up over 19 seasons, he'll need to maintain his current pace for another 12 seasons—a most unlikely scenario.

2. John Randle leads the list of 157 Vikings who had at least half a sack. In more than 11 seasons with Minnesota, he totaled 114 sacks. He added another 23.5 sacks over three years with the Seattle Seahawks and is tied for ninth in career sacks in the NFL. He's the only defensive tackle in the top five in career sacks for the Vikings.

3. In his first season (1963) with the Vikings, field goal specialist Fred Cox also punted the ball 70 times with an average of 38.7 yards per attempt.

4. One writer opined: "Brett Favre's consecutive games played streak is significantly more impressive than Cal Ripken's. He played in every game from 1992 to 2010. It's an incredible rarity for a quarterback to even play 18 seasons. Start every game and play through the type of injuries Favre has suffered? Absolutely ridiculous."

5. Minnesota record-setter Sammie White worked as a receivers coach (1998-2003 and 2007-09) and offensive coordinator (2004-06) at his alma mater, Grambling. During that time, his team won six Western Division titles and five SWAC championships.

6. Don Hultz holds the NFL record for the most opponents' fumbles recovered in a season (9) in 1963, which was his rookie year.

7. Early in his career, punter Greg Coleman earned the nickname "Coffin Corner" because of his ability to land his kicks near the corner of the playing field where the end zone and sidelines meet. He holds the career mark in Minnesota for most punts, with 720.

8. In 1985, George "Buster" Rhymes set an NFL single-season record for kick return yardage, with 1,345 yards. The league record has since been broken, but the total stood as a Vikings franchise record until broken by Cordarrelle Patterson in the final game of the 2013 season.

9. After seven seasons with the Vikings, center Kirk Lowdermilk was signed by the Indianapolis Colts in 1993 for the then-highest contract ($6 million+) ever given to an offensive lineman.

10. One dubious Super Bowl record the Vikings were involved in was the lowest number of total points in a half, which was two. After a single safety against Fran Tarkenton, the Steelers went into the locker room with a 2-0 lead in 1975.

CHAPTER 13:

BRING ON THE RIVALS

QUIZ TIME!

1. In a 2002 contest against rivals Green Bay, the Vikings were shocked that a certain Packers player raced across the field to join the fracas before the final play was over and smacked a Minnesota player in the face. Who was the culprit?

   a. Desmond Howard

   b. Cletidus Hunt

   c. Mark Ingram

   d. Darren Sharper

2. "What had grown between the Bears and Vikings was true hostility, with little of the respect that the Bears and Packers had managed." What year does this refer to?

   a. 1985

   b. 1995

   c. 2003

   d. 2013

3. "To say there's some bad blood between the teams might be an understatement. I've always said football's a tough sport. It's not a nice man's game." Which Green Bay player said this about the rivalry with Minnesota in 2002?

    a. Timothy Brown

    b. Donald Driver

    c. Brett Favre

    d. Josh Heupel

4. What was the amount of the fines that both Minnesota's Chris Hovan and Green Bay's Favre received for trash-talking in another 2002 matchup?

    a. $5,000

    b. $25,000

    c. $50,000

    d. $75,000

5. The rivalry between the Vikings and the Pack has been described as "regional, hard-hitting, and _____." What's missing?

    a. backstabbing

    b. barnstorming

    c. bitter

    d. bizarre

6. The University of Minnesota also has a tense rivalry against the University of Wisconsin. What item is given each year to the winner of the contest?

    a. A 10-pound block of cheddar cheese

    b. A 25-pound bag of Minnesota wild rice

c. Free Friday night fish-fry for 100 guests

d. Paul Bunyan's axe

7. "The Vikings as a team is not hated. The Viking fans, however, have become unreasonably unruly and disrespectful. It's embarrassing. The Vikings fans have the highest arrest record at Lambeau Field (Green Bay's home)." Who said this?

a. Green Bay evening news

b. Green Bay police chief

c. Green Bay psychologist

d. Wayne Sargent, Green Bay Packers fanatic

8. In the 2004 playoffs, Randy Moss caught his second touchdown pass, and then walked over to the Lambeau Field faithful and faked a mooning gesture. Howard Cosell quipped, "That is a disgusting act."

a. True

b. False

9. How many players have played for both Minnesota and Green Bay?

a. 12

b. 17

c. 24

d. 33

10. The hatred in Minnesota may run a little deeper than it does in Green Bay. As Marshall Eriksen said about letting _____ play football, "The Green Bay Packers have been proving that for years." What's missing?

a. animals

b. fools

c. girls

d. sissies

11. Which rival is geographically closest to Minneapolis?

    a. Chicago

    b. Cleveland

    c. Detroit

    d. Green Bay

12. How many times did Green Bay, under legendary coach Vince Lombardi, beat the Vikings in their first 10 games from 1961 to 1965?

    a. 10

    b. 9

    c. 7

    d. 6

13. When Brett Favre feuded with Green Bay management in 2008, he was traded to a team with the stipulation that they'd cough up multiple draft picks if he was ever traded to an NFC North team (presumably the Vikings). Which team received Favre?

    a. Buffalo Bills

    b. New England Patriots

    c. New York Giants

    d. New York Jets

14. In 1972, the Packers visited Minnesota on the last day of the season, scored 23 unanswered points, and clinched the division. How many consecutive years previously had Minnesota been division champs?

    a. 6
    b. 4
    c. 3
    d. 2

15. At the end of 1993, Minnesota made an improbable comeback in the last seconds behind the wizardry of Jim McMahon to beat Green Bay. Fuad Reveiz kicked his fifth field goal of the game to seal the deal.

    a. True
    b. False

16. On October 5, 1995, rookie Randy Moss strutted his stuff on *Monday Night Football* as Minnesota pounded the Packers at Lambeau Field, 37-24, ending an 18-game home win streak for the Pack. Which Vikings kicker drilled three field goals in that game?

    a. Gary Anderson
    b. Dan Bailey
    c. Fred Cox
    d. Blair Walsh

17. In the 2005 Minnesota win at Green Bay, including the infamous Moss "mooning" episode, which Vikings quarterback tossed four touchdown passes?

a. Daunte Culpepper

b. Randall Cunningham

c. Sean Mannion

d. Fran Tarkenton

18. In 2008, the Vikings snuck by the Pack in the Hubert H. Humphrey Metrodome, 28-27. Who was responsible for a clinching safety against Green Bay's Aaron Rodgers?

a. Jared Allen

b. Chad Greenway

c. Benny Sapp

d. Madieu Williams

19. *Monday Night Football* earned the highest ratings in cable television history on October 5, 2009, when the Vikings hosted the Packers in Favre's first game against his former team. What was the final score of that Vikings victory?

a. 36-28

b. 30-23

c. 30-10

d. 24-6

20. When Vikings linebacker Anthony Barr made his controversial hit on Aaron Rodgers in 2017, the quarterback was forced to leave the game. Who replaced Rogers and couldn't manage to guide the Pack to the playoffs?

a. Tim Boyle

b. Joe Callahan

c. Taysom Hill

d. Brett Hundley

QUIZ ANSWERS

1. B – Cletidus Hunt

2. B – 1995

3. C – Brett Favre

4. A – $5,000

5. A – backstabbing

6. D – Paul Bunyan's axe

7. D – Wayne Sargent, Green Bay Packers fanatic

8. B – False (The announcer was Joe Buck.)

9. B – 17

10. C – Girls

11. D – Green Bay

12. B – 9

13. D – New York Jets

14. B – 4

15. A – True

16. A – Gary Anderson

17. A – Daunte Culpepper

18. A – Jared Allen

19. B – 30-23

20. D – Brett Hundley

DID YOU KNOW?

1. Every time the Vikings and Green Bay Packers play, there is a little extra on the line. The first time these two teams played was in October 1961, with the Packers coming away with a 33-7 victory.

2. The Vikings and Packers have squared off 119 times, and the Packers lead the all-time series 62-54-3. The Vikings own the longest win streak in the rivalry, beating the Packers seven straight times from 1975 to 1978.

3. Minnesota and the Chicago Bears have faced off 118 times in their history, with the Vikings leading the series 60-56-2. The win by the Bears in the 1995 playoffs was the only time the two teams have met in the postseason. The longest win streak by either team is held by the Vikings, who won eight straight games from 1972 to 1978.

4. In the 2009 season, the Saints became a Minnesota rival. The two teams faced off in the NFC Championship game, which the Saints won. Afterward, there were claims that a bounty system had been put in place by the Saints to possibly hurt Vikings players, including quarterback Brett Favre.

5. The Vikings are rivals with the Detroit Lions simply because they play in the same division. Minnesota beat Detroit 13 times in a row from 1968 to 1974, while the Lions have only had a winning record against Minnesota

in one decade. That was in the 1960s when they went 9-7-2.

6. Since winning 35-15 in Kansas City on December 14, 1974, Minnesota has been back merely three times in the past 37 years and lost each time. The only teams the Vikings have longer road losing streaks against are the New York Jets and Baltimore/Indianapolis Colts, where they've never won.

7. "The place can get extremely loud," said Vikings special teams coach Mike Priefer, who held the same position in Kansas City from 2006 to 2008. "The only place that's as loud, other than Mall of America Field, would be Seattle. That's what makes it intimidating."

8. Hank Stram's legacy was forged with a 23-7 victory over the Vikings in Super Bowl IV, the final game between the AFL and NFL before the 1970 merger. NFL Films captured Stram's bravado on the sideline when producers decided to wire a head coach with a mic for the first time.

9. The Minnesota-Green Bay rivalry in a nutshell: "Bud Grant hassling Vince Lombardi's teams in the 1960s, the house of horrors that was the Metrodome in the 1990s, or current Viking fans' obsession with replaying Anthony Barr's hit on Aaron Rodgers in 2017. There's been plenty of nastiness to go around when these two teams get together."

10. The Vikings-Bears animosity is not only between teams but also individual players. One Bears defensive lineman

declared that his most hated opponent was Minnesota right tackle Tim Irwin: "He's a guy that, if I ran over him with a car, I'd back up over him to make sure I got him."

CONCLUSION

If we've done our job well, you are now chock-full of new facts about your favorite NFL team, the Minnesota Vikings. Whether it's the notable players who hold franchise records or behind-the-scenes information about how some of your favorite stars arrived in Minnesota, we hope you enjoyed this trip down memory lane and through the rich history of the Vikings.

We've done our best to cover it all for you, from their first-ever NFL championship in 1969 through Super Bowl trips in 1970, 1974, 1975, and 1977 to some of the darker days in the franchise's history.

In the Super Bowl era, Minnesota has had its fair share of highlights, but there have been some lean years in the Twin Cities as well. Throughout the Vikes' storied history, some of the best players ever to play the game have done it with Minnesota. They might not have as many Lombardi Trophies as you'd like, but the Vikings are a large part of the fabric of the league we know and love.

This book is designed for you, the fans, to embrace your favorite team and feel closer to them. Maybe you weren't totally familiar with franchise history. Perhaps you were unaware of the early success Minnesota had in the NFL. Maybe you didn't realize just how shrewdly the Vikings used and traded their draft picks to pick up legendary talents.

Or perhaps we couldn't stump you at all because you're the ultimate super-fan! No matter how well you did on the quizzes, we hope we captured the spirit of the purple and gold Vikings and inspired even more pride in your team.

The Vikings are still one of the winningest teams in league history, and as always, they'll continue to give it their all. "Go Vikings, run up the score! You'll hear us yell for more. . . Skol, Vikings, let's go! Skol, Vikings!" as the fight song goes. We're still working on a great new catch phrase for next year. Stay tuned!

Made in the USA
Monee, IL
18 December 2022

22808067R00074